Maximizing Your Time Until It's Your Turn

Learning To Serve With Purpose Without Seeking Position

Marcus Ellison

Maximizing Your Time Until It's Your Turn
Learning To Serve With Purpose Without Seeking Position
By Marcus Ellison
© 2023 Marcus Ellison
ISBN: 978-1-937514-25-9

Printed by: Camden House Books, LLC
Contact: 918-361-6654
Distributed by: www.GetMyNewBook.com
Edition: 4864-2

Editorial Director: Dr. Larry Keefauver
www.doctorlarry.org
Text Design: Lisa Simpson

All rights reserved solely by the author. The author guarantees all contents are original and do not infringe upon the legal rights of any other person or work. No part of this book may be reproduced, stored in a retrieval system, or transmitted in any form or by any means without expressed written permission of the author.

All quotes, unless otherwise noted, are from the New King James Version. Copyright 1979, 1980, 1982 by Thomas Nelson, Inc. Used by permission. All rights reserved.

Scriptures marked NIV are taken from the HOLY BIBLE, NEW INTERNATIONAL VERSION,. Copyright © 1973, 1978, 1984 by International Bible Society. Used by permission of Zondervan Publishing House. All rights reserved.

Scriptures marked KJV are taken from The Holy Bible, King James Version. Copyright © 1972 by Thomas Nelson Inc., Camden, New Jersey 08103.

Scripture marked MSG are taken from The Message. Published by permission. Originally published by NavPress in English as THE MESSAGE: The Bible in Contemporary Language copyright 2002 by Eugene Peterson. All rights reserved.

Scriptures marked NLT are taken from the Holy Bible, New Living Translation, copyright © 1996, 2004, 2007 by Tyndale House Foundation. Used by permission of Tyndale House Publishers, Inc., Carol Stream, Illinois 60188. All rights reserved.

Scriptures marked ESV are taken from the ESV® Bible (The Holy Bible, English Standard Version®) copyright © 2001 by Crossway, a publishing ministry of Good News Publishers. ESV® Text Edition: 2011.

All rights reserved.

DEDICATION

This Book Is Dedicated To My Grandmothers:

Ruther Louise Page and Josie Jenkins

Acknowledgments

I am truly grateful for all those who have poured into my life and ministry throughout the years. I thank God for calling me into the ministry and giving me the gifts and talents to be used for His Glory.

To My lovely wife, Tasheka Morris-Ellison: thank you for your continued support and love throughout the years. You have been there through it all. Thank you for being so patient throughout the process. You are truly a God-sent helpmate.

To My lovely daughter Morgan Ellison: you are the reason I do what I do. I want you to enjoy the fullness of life and all it has to offer. My desire is to leave an inheritance that money can't buy and establish a solid foundation for you to build upon.

To My Mother, Marilyn Holly: thank you for being an example of strength and determination. Thank you for setting the standard for excellence. You are truly an inspiration.

To Pastor Tommy L. Carr of the Zion Hill Baptist Church of Farmerville, La: I am forever grateful for you introducing me to Christian Education. I am honored to call you, My Pastor.

To My Family: thank you for the steadfast support and unyielding love from day one. Thank you for being instrumental in my growth and development.

To All Of My Pastors Throughout the Years: B.J Washington, Tommy Carr, H. Bruce Maxwell, Bishop Joseph Walker, and C.L. Hicks Sr: Thank you all for all of the conversations, inspiration, and motivation to keep serving the God who called me into this ministry. I am forever grateful for the time, training, and teaching.

To My Best Friend, Michael Singleton: Thank you for being a friend in adversity. You are a blessing to my ministry and to me as a person.

To the Mt. Olive Baptist Church; Thank you for giving me the opportunity to serve as pastor for these 10 years. You are the best!

TABLE OF CONTENTS

Introduction 9

Chapter 1   Are You Serving with Purpose
or Seeking a Position? 13

Chapter 2   What Time Is It? 25

Chapter 3   Help! My Anointing Does Not Match
My Assignment 35

Chapter 4   Your Gift Will Make Room for You 43

Chapter 5   Why Am I Here? 51

Chapter 6   Please Be Patient with Me… God Is at Work 59

Chapter 7   Handling Applause and Adversity –
The Price of Popularity 75

Final Word   It's Worth the Wait 85

About the Author 94

Endnotes 95

Introduction

Prepared for Purpose

In September of 2011, the Mt. Olive B.C. of Greenwood began the search for a new pastor. They needed someone to fill this vacant position. Who would be the twelfth pastor in their church's 132-year history? Where would they find the next shepherd of their congregation? Although they did not know, God had a man in mind. The church spent ten weeks in prayer and commenced to ask God to send them a pastor with four specific qualities: (1) Married, (2) Young and Energetic, (3) Seminary Trained, and (4) Not Currently Serving as a Pastor. The church with prayer and supplication with thanksgiving, let their requests be made known unto God. As God said about David, "I have found David the son of Jesse, a man after mine own heart, which shall fulfil all my will." He prepared his servant for the position. As the Mt. Olive Baptist Church was in the process of figuring it out, God had already worked it out.

I married the love of my life, TaSheka Morris-Ellison on July 21, 2001. We moved to Nashville, TN, in 2002 where our daughter, Morgan was born. We had some difficult days early in the marriage, but God held it together. Why did God hold it together? Why did God not allow it to fall apart? Because His purpose was larger than our problems. He was preparing me to fulfill the church's desire to have a pastor who was married. It was in Nashville that I accepted my calling into the ministry in 2003. The foundation of family and ministry were established in Nashville for an assignment in Greenwood.

As God would have it, I was blessed to sit under the leadership of Bishop Joseph Walker III and observe his zeal and passion for young adult ministry. I witnessed him reach a generation that most have labeled unreachable. He was intentional in his approach to reach the millennials. In 2004, I transitioned to the Lake Providence Baptist Church and was placed over the Young Adult ministry. I began to teach Sunday School and served closely with Pastor H. Bruce Maxwell. I was receiving the training necessary to fulfill the church's desire to have a young energetic pastor who could reach the millennials. The training in Nashville was preparing me for the assignment in Greenwood.

In 2006, we transitioned back home to Shreveport, LA where I served on staff at the Avenue Baptist Church under the leadership of Clarence L. Hicks. This was a great opportunity to put into practice all that I had observed under the previous administrations. Pastor Hicks was a seminary-trained pastor who was passionate about preachers getting the necessary training to rightly divide the Word of God. I was enrolled at the BMA seminary in Jacksonville, TX. I traveled back and forth for three hours twice a week until I received my Bachelors Degree in May of 2009 and a Master's Degree in May 2010. I later enrolled in Liberty University and received my Masters of Divinity in 2011. God had given me grace and favor to receive some quality seminary training to fulfill the church's desire to have a seminary-trained pastor. While serving as an Associate Minister at Avenue, God was preparing me for my assignment in Greenwood.

I served on the Avenue Baptist Church staff from February 2006 until June of 2012. In those years, I served as assistant to Pastor Hicks. Through the years, we were able to make an impact on the Kingdom through team ministry. In 2010, I was a candidate for a church in Grambling, LA. This was a church that was close to two college campuses. It was a great opportunity for me to work in the area of my passion. I was one of the final two candidates. The tension and anxiety of becoming a first-time pastor was great. I began to seek God for confirmation that I was making the right decision. The Monday night before my final preaching assignment at the church, God spoke in a still small voice, "This is not the assignment." That was not the answer I was hoping for, but I had peace with the decision. I called the Search Committee chairman and stated that I would not show up for my preaching engagement that Sunday. He expressed his disappointment but said the church would vote anyway. In an extremely close vote, I was not selected as the new pastor of the church. I was not disappointed, but I did ask God, *why*? Now I know! God had to keep me as an associate minister because the search committee in Greenwood asked God for a minister who was not pastoring YET. God closed a door that was appealing to keep me in position to walk into the door of assignment. Although what you desire today may be appealing, is it your assignment?

Psalms 37:23 declares, "The steps of a good man are ordered by the Lord and He delights in his way." God was ordering my steps not for the position, but for a purpose. **Too often we seek to find the perfect position instead of allowing God to order our steps.** God was preparing me for purpose that aligned with the position. My task was not to get weary in welldoing, and trust that in due season I would reap.

Chapter 1

ARE YOU SERVING WITH PURPOSE OR SEEKING A POSITION?

On my journey to becoming the Pastor of the Mt. Olive Baptist Church, I was blessed to receive quality seminary training. By the grace of God and the support of my church, I earned four seminary degrees from two quality institutions. Throughout my years of seminary training, I never took a course concerning Associate Ministry. I took classes on Pastoral Leadership, Pastoral Counseling, and Pastoral Development. I took several courses on sermon preparation; but not one course on how to serve as an associate. I received the necessary classes for THE POSITION. However, I was not prepared for the wait. I was prepared for a position that I did not have or maybe never be called to fulfill!

This is one of the reasons that churches are struggling to experience sustained growth. The swift growth of churches has become too large of a challenge for solo pastors. For this growth and development to be sustainable, it requires team members who are committed to a common goal and purpose. Pastors are discovering that many associates ministers cannot provide the necessary support for team ministry. Often associate ministers have not been properly trained to serve without the position of Pastor. Any church or ministry organization, or kingdom business for that matter, that seeks to increase its impact and its effectiveness needs to train and develop leaders. The task of training and developing a support, servant-leadership team is challenging because many associates are seeking the satisfaction of becoming the pastor. Many associates are not content with serving in this role and they are not trained to serve in this role.

After careful observation, this mindset is not exclusive to church and ministry, but in all societies. Many people feel fulfillment can only be found in top-level positions and promotions. They do not understand purpose can be fulfilling. When purpose becomes the object of fulfillment, one begins to develop a different mindset about serving for a greater goal. Influence does not require position when purpose is the primary focus. The position or the title is not essential to make an impact. You do not need to be recognized to make a difference.

Purpose vs. Position

The Associate Minister is not viewed as a desired position in my calling. Instead, it is viewed as a stop on the journey to Senior Pastor. This is dangerous! Many associates fail to take advantage of the opportunities provided for growth, training, development, and maturation in ministry. Popular culture suggests titles, positions, and promotions are the real signs of success. Therefore, many people are Position Driven rather than Purpose Driven.

Many people are position-driven instead of being purpose-driven.

While serving as an associate minister, I discovered that personal satisfaction was not the primary goal in ministry. Serving God and being faithful is the ultimate goal. This is a difficult task because many associates struggle to find fulfillment and significance in this role. I can admit, there is a struggle to sustain focus, patience, and contentment while serving in the second chair or a support position of leadership. Although the task is difficult, the rewards are incredibly beneficial.

After serving in the role of associate minister for eight years, I transitioned into the role of senior pastor in July of 2012. The training and preparation provided in the associate minister's role enabled my current church family and me to experience tremendous growth and development in the first ten years of my tenure. I noticed that many who are called into the ministry approach the role of the associate minister from different perspectives. Most associate ministers are not aware of the impact their perspective has on the congregation and the growth of the minister. Not every associate minister is focused on their current assignment.

THE CHANGE BEGINS WITH PERSPECTIVE

Many people are seeking fulfillment in positions rather than finding fulfillment in purpose.

**As you minister and serve others,
seek fulfillment in God's purpose not your position.**

The root of the problem lies in the realm of perspective. Our society encourages employees to move up the corporate ladder and become executives. This mindset is a temptation for many associate ministers who feel the only way to measure success is to become a pastor. One associate minister says, "The younger generation is being trained more on the business model of looking at steppingstones and career moves rather than hearing from God." Becoming a senior pastor is not the ultimate goal. The ultimate goal should be doing the will of God. Your position or your title does not determine your value to the Body of Christ. God will reward faithfulness and fruitfulness, regardless of position or status.

In his book, *The 360° Leader*, John Maxwell deals with the position myth. He suggests, "the number one misconception people have about leadership is the belief that leadership comes simply from having a position or title."[1] He argues that authentic leadership has more to do with a disposition than a position. This is valuable when it comes to shifting the perspective about the role of an associate minister. One does not have to have a position to find fulfillment and contentment in ministry. After careful and considerable observations, four perspectives were noticed among associate ministers.

Is Your Position a Stepping-Stone?

The first perspective is to view the role as a "*stepping-stone*" to the next assignment. This person views their current assignment as seemingly insignificant, but necessary to get to their intended or desired destination. This person does not maximize this opportunity because they view it as literally a "temporary waste of time." They consider this role as an internship necessary to transition into their next assignment. Their mindset is: "I am only here until I get my own church or the current pastor leaves." They have the mentality, "I do not have to get too involved here. I do not need to know or support the vision. I am not going to be here forever." This mentality is shortsighted, and it limits the possibility of acquiring what God has for them to learn in this particular place and at this particular time. Daniel Threlfall, in his article, *Pastoral Promotion: How Climbing Up Will Take You Down*, states, "discontent with their supposedly small-minded and backward congregations, some pastors are surreptitiously sending out resumes, dropping hints, phoning up friends, and keeping one eye open for their lucky break to a big-time church."[2] With this perspective, there is the danger of not developing the necessary skills needed for the next assignment. Don't view it as a "stepping stone." Every opportunity is critical.

Are You Happy Where You Are?

The second perspective is the "*I am just happy to be here*" perspective. This person is not concerned with doing ministry or impacting the kingdom. They desire to sit in the pulpit and be noticed. They are excited to have a title and a position of prominence. They have found a sense of contentment with just being included in the staff directory and labeled as an associate minister of the church. They are not faithful to the ministry and are not fully committed to kingdom success. This person shows up on Sunday and is excited to be noticed. They have misjudged contentment for complacency. They are satisfied with waiting around for their next opportunity to preach but not seeking an opportunity to serve in some capacity.

Billy Hornsby suggests that this person feels the position makes him or her significant. Hornsby states, "significance has nothing to do with position, but rather service and serving is the only path to significance."[3] Some have even asked, "if I am not going to preach, what else is there to do?" They fail to understand that there are many things needed to help fulfill the mandate of making disciples. These assignments may include leading worship service, teaching Bible study or Sunday School, visiting the sick, assisting with the youth and children, new member follow-up, evangelism and outreach, and promoting the vision of the pastor. There is more than enough work to do if you are serious and committed to ministry and not just a position. Ministry is not a place of comfort or complacency. It is a place of service.

LOOKING FOR A NEW ASSIGNMENT?

The third perspective is the one who is continuously *looking for a new assignment*. This person has a resume in every vacant church and is continually seeking new opportunities to become a pastor. They are enamored by the position of Pastor but are not willing to serve as an associate. This person feels they have the necessary gifts, talents, and abilities to serve as senior pastor and are not willing to settle for an associate role. Their mindset is, "I did not accept my calling to sit under someone else." Their only desire is to preach and lead a flock. They have no interest in subordinate leadership positions. This person is not dependable, accountable, or faithful. They desire position without sacrifice.

Are You Serving with Purpose or Seeking a Position?

The pastor and congregation can never build a sense of cohesion among the pastoral leadership team with associate ministers who share this perspective.

Dr. David Hopewell suggests, "This person hinders the vision and work at their current church, and also hinders his or her own destiny."[4] This person is continually visiting other churches seeking positions and opportunities. Dr. Martin Hawkins refers to this person as the "unintentional assistant." He says, "Trying to keep this person on staff will usually only do a disservice to him and the staff he serves because he will continually butt his head against the restrictions placed on his calling, his passion, and even his personality."[5] Their attention is fixed on position rather than purpose.

ARE YOU MAXIMIZING THE OPPORTUNITY?

The final perspective is the associate who *maximizes the opportunity* to mature, develop, and grow as a leader. This person views the role of the associate minister as an assignment by God that serves a purpose. This individual is committed to assisting the pastor in bringing about the unity and maturity within the body of Christ. He desires to fulfill God's call on his life in a way that brings glory to God. He is in full alignment with the vision of the pastor. This person is passionate about organizing and implementing programs that effectively impact the congregation. This viewpoint understands and embraces the opportunity to grow in subordinate leadership without the burden of senior pastor pressure. This person sees his value and worth to the pastor and congregation. This person sees the high potential of the associate minister position. It is not just a temporary position. The associate minister role is a place where one can exercise their gifts and abilities. Their joy is seeing others succeed.

> **A shepherd's desire is
> to equip others to succeed.**

An effective leader does not view other leaders as competitors for the top spot but views every member as co-laborers in the ministry. They have a "bloom where you are planted" mentality. There is an excellent understanding that second-chair leadership provides an excellent opportunity to be a learner. Learning is the only thing that ensures growth, and it continues to feed your inner desire for improvement. These experiences can help teach, train, and prepare the minister to serve God's people, maintain integrity in ministry, and allow making mistakes behind the scenes.

After carefully observing these various perspectives, the mindset toward the role of the associate minister must shift toward the fourth perspective. This perspective provides fantastic possibilities for associate ministers to grow into the leader that God has called them to be. The associate position will become a place of observation. The associate minister could have his eyes opened to the responsibility and accountability of responsible pastoral work and view the role of the pastor differently. Many associates only see the glamour of Sunday morning preaching, celebrations and generous honorariums. Too many fail to see the behind-the-scenes burdens involved in leadership. David Hopewell points out, "If we truly understood all the long hours of prayer and study, hours away from family members, the misunderstandings, accusations, ingratitude, and everything else that goes along with the job of the pastor, we may no longer want it."[6]

Are You Serving with Purpose or Seeking a Position?

Maintaining the proper perspective could also provide the associate minister an opportunity to experience a season of preparation. While serving in the second chair, I was able to receive more formal seminary training. The position allowed me the time and resources to be able to go and receive training that was necessary for ministry. In his book, "The Making of a Leader," Dr. J. Robert Clinton suggests, "If you know that God will be developing you over a lifetime, you will most likely stay for the whole ride."[7] The right perspective will enable associate ministers to see the "Big Picture" of what God is doing in their lives. In this time of preparation, the right perspective will enable God to begin to transform the minister into an effective leader without the title or position. Approaching the position with the proper perspective will enable the associate minister to have a positive influence that will ultimately benefit the congregation. This influence can only be done if the associate minister has the right perspective on their role.

So, the question becomes: *How does one shift their perspective toward service, submission, and success in my current role?* This book is designed to offer some biblical principles that will encourage and equip you to serve effectively in your current role and prayerfully present a model that will shift the perspective from position toward purpose; regardless of your occupation.

To achieve this goal, this book will examine the life of King David. He exemplified patience, trust, and fulfilling God's purpose. After being anointed to be king at an early age, David served as a shepherd with a king's mindset. He continued to serve until God changed his assignment. David served faithfully under Saul's leadership for more than fifteen years. He was able to grow, mature, and develop into what God's purpose was for him while fulfilling his assignment as a subordinate leader.

How was David able to find contentment serving under Saul's leadership? There are seven principles that this research will highlight that are gleaned from 1 Samuel. These fundamental principles include: (1) being faithful over the simple assignments, (2) the development of your gift in private, (3) being patient through the process of preparation, (4) learning to handle early success, (5) developing healthy relationships, (6) resolving conflict, and (7) knowing when to leave the current assignment. These principles were exhibited in various stages of the life of King David.

Walk with me through this journey and you will discover that there is joy in the journey.

Ask yourself...

- *Which perspective do you identify with and why?*
- *Has your perspective changed over the years?*
- *What influenced your perspective?*
- *Are you open to changing your perspective?*

Discipline Yourself...

Serving with Purpose begins with discipline which comes from the word "disciple." We are discipled by Jesus Christ through the guidance of the Holy Spirit. A disciple follows the example of words and deeds filled with Spirit and Truth. The overarching focus or perspective of a disciple is "fixing your eyes on Jesus" who begins and ends everything we do with trusting and obeying Him. We have His perspective—we see everything in life from His perspective...

The godly servant-leader sees Everyone & Everything From God's Perspective!

Set your minds on things that are above, not on things that are on earth.
(Colossians 3:2)

Chapter 2

WHAT TIME IS IT?

*"There is a time for everything,
and a season for every activity under heaven…"*
(Ecclesiastes 3:1 NIV)

In every generation, a group of aspiring church leaders are waiting on "***THEIR TURN***" and asking…

- When is it *my turn* to preach?
- When is it *my turn* to pastor?
- When is it *my turn* to lead?
- When is it *my turn* to be in charge, in control, and in command?

Because they are so concerned about ***their turn***; often they don't understand **THE TIME**. Therefore, valuable time is wasted, waiting on ***their turn***. In their mind, they are ready for ***their turn***. They are ready for the spotlight. They are ready for the stage. They are ready for the status. They are ready for the title. *But, are they prepared?* God has designated a time to prepare you for **your turn**.

People who don't understand **this time** or season of preparation will plant dangerous seed. I can recall several Sundays as an associate minister, when I would be asked, "When are you going to get *your own church*? You are ready to lead. It's **your turn** to be in charge." I don't think they were speaking from a perspective of evil or malicious intent. They just assumed that because I was an associate for a **certain amount time** and was gifted in a few areas, it should be **MY TURN NOW!**

The danger with planting these seeds is that an aspiring leader begins to see others getting **their turn**. Now they become emotional about the elevation of others. So, the flesh begins to ponder the question: "**when will it be my turn?**" Hearing such questions and seeing others promoted, I soon developed an expectation that **my turn** was next, if not now. This expectation eventually led to frustration. In my mind, I was just as gifted as those selected to pastoral positions. The constant questions about **MY TURN**, led me to become frustrated with **MY TIME**.

God never designed time to be wasted. Time should be maximized. In fact, one way to translate the Hebrew word for time is: *a container filled with limitless opportunities*. Therefore, to push or rush through the "now moment in time" is to miss much of what God may have for you. Ephesians 5:15-17 reads, "Be careful, then, how you live, not as unwise but as wise, making the most of every opportunity, because the days are evil. Therefore, do not be foolish, but understand what the Lord's will is…."

The Greek language has two different words for "time." One is the word, "Chronos," from which we derive our word *chronology*.

What Time Is It?

"Chronos" is time measured in seconds, minutes, hours, days, and years. But the Greek language has another word for time. It is the word, *Kairos*. A *Kairos* moment is a moment of opportunity in due or the right time or appointed time/season. It is time measured not in seconds or minutes but in terms of an opportunity seized or lost.

Many leaders feel they are ready based on the clocks and calendars. Their mindset says, my length of service, not my loyalty, has earned my elevation or promotion. If you are not careful the calendar will continue to change without any growth and development. This mindset will view your current season as "just killing time." In reality, you are wasting time and squandering God-given opportunities.

God operates in *kairos* moments, "the appointed time." *Kairos* is a distinct time, the chosen time. It's God's fixed and appointed time specifically for His purposes. In God's sovereign *kairos* time, He interacts, intervenes, or even interrupts *chronos* time according to His perfect will. *Kairos* is a specific time when something significant happens, where history is made, and destiny is launched from the invisible into the visible.

It is important to understand the times and seasons in your life. God has an opportune moment, a suitable moment, and a favorable moment planned for you. This reality helps you to wait patiently and fulfill purpose. Understanding the times gives insight into what to do and when to do it. There were several people who demonstrated an understanding of a "KAIROS MOMENT." This can be seen in several passages throughout Scripture. Here Are A Few Benefits of Understanding the Times.

WHEN YOU UNDERSTAND THE *KAIROS* TIME, YOU CAN REMAIN FOCUSED

*² Now the Jews' Feast of Tabernacles was at hand.
³ His brothers therefore said to Him, "Depart from here and go into Judea, that Your disciples also may see the works that You are doing.
⁴ For no one does anything in secret while he himself seeks to be known openly. If You do these things, show Yourself to the world."
⁵ For even His brothers did not believe in Him. ⁶ Then Jesus said to them, "My time has not yet come, but your time is always ready.
⁷ The world cannot hate you, but it hates Me because I testify of it that its works are evil. ⁸ You go up to this feast.
I am not yet going up to this feast,
for My time has not yet fully come."*
(John 7:2-8)

In John 7, Jesus' brothers were pushing Him to promote Himself. They encouraged Him to transition to a specific place to demonstrate His status. They said to Him, "Depart from here and go there to show them something (John 7:3)." Why would you stay here? You need to be at a place to be recognized. Jesus' response is one of significance: "My TIME has not yet come...." Understanding the value of *kairos* moments will keep you focused on the task at hand.

The flesh's temptation is to GO and SHOW, but staying focused on the assignment says,
Stay and Grow.

This could also be seen in John 2, when Jesus was invited to a wedding in Cana of Galilee. The bridal party ran out of wine and Jesus' mother informed Jesus of the situation. He responded by saying, "Woman, what does your concern have to do with Me? My hour has not yet come." Understanding the time, enabled Him to stay focused on the task at hand.

If you are not careful, you will find yourself being pushed into prominence and seeking positions without going through the period of preparation. That is a recipe for disaster. The enemy will provide a temptation, "if you are who you say are… then do something to prove it. Understanding the times and seasons will empower you to remain focused on the task at hand.

**Focus on what God wants NOW,
Don't be distracted by your wants and desires!**

When You Understand the Time, You Can Respond by Faith

Abraham was given a promise and a favorable moment for a child. Although the calendar said, "Too Late." God promised, *there's still time*. Abraham trusted God that He would keep his promise of a child at the appointed time. Abraham received a promise from God that he would have a son through Sarah. He was promised that his descendants would be as numerous as the stars in the sky. He then moved into a 24-year *chronos* season of having to persevere and ***respond by faith***.

After so many years in the *chronos* season, Abraham and Sarah laughed at this prospect. Abraham even tried to create shortcuts to alter the time. The Word says that Abraham believed God and trusted that God was able to perform his promise. By **Faith**, Abraham and Sarah moved from *chronos* into *kairos*. Understanding the times and seasons will give you the hope you need to trust God in testing season.

When You Understand the Time, You Remember Not to Forget

Esther was raised for a specific time… She was prepared for her *kairos* Moment. *Kairos* is the moment of decision, the moment of action, the moment of change. Germans speak of *Der Tag*—a specially appointed time that calls for a decision. Esther faced such a moment when she boldly turned toward great opposition that threatened not only her life, but all of Israel.

In a *kairos* moment, she courageously said, "I and my young women will also fast likewise. Only then would I dare go to the king since it is not allowed by law, and if I perish, I perish" (Esther 4:16b). She displayed a boldness to believe despite the danger and opposition.

Although she had a great position, she was prepared for a specific moment. When the moment arrived, a decision had to be made. *Kairos* moments require a decision to be made that will have an impact beyond self, an impact for now and eternity! The decision had to be made despite the danger. Mordecai reminded her "You were made for such a time as this!" Understanding God's timing is often one of the keys to taking the proper action. It would have been comfortable to remain in the position of queen, but her *kairos* moment reminded her not to forget who she was, who her people were and who her God was—the Great I AM. It was her appointed *kairos moment* to make the decision that shaped Israel's destiny according to God's plan.

When You Understand the Time, You Are Ready for a Spiritual Warfare

The enemy knows God has a destiny and plan for your life. Therefore, he will attack at every opportune time to defeat, distract, discourage, and detour us from our destiny. When Jesus was applauded by the Spirit in Matthew 3, "This is my beloved Son in whom I am well pleased," the enemy was preparing to attack in Matthew 4. Jesus was able to stand firm on the Word of God and defeat the enemy. But Luke records that the enemy left Him until an **opportune time**. He did not throw in the towel or wave the white flag. He just said, "I will be back". When you understand the Kairos moments you remain ready for spiritual warfare.

You Will Be Rewarded for Faithfulness

God rewards us at the proper time. Galatians 6:9 declares, "And let us not grow weary while doing good, for in due season we shall reap if we do not lose heart." God has promised something special to those who endure the process of preparation season.

In Luke 12:42, Jesus asks an intriguing question, "Who then is that faithful and wise steward, whom his master will make ruler over his household, to give them their portion of food in due season?" Our responsibility is to be faithful with our assignment. God will reward in due season.

Therefore, as we go through the season of preparation, we must be mindful of the *chronos* and *kairos* moments. Be conscious of your minutes, hours, days, weeks, months, and years. Time is valuable. Time is a container of limitless opportunities. Being consciously aware and a good steward of your *chronos* will prepare you to maximize your *kairos*. There must be a mental shift in your evaluation of time. You will discover that not every second holds the same worth. Some moments are more valuable. Therefore, instead of **pursuing** every opportunity that becomes available; **sense** the best one that God is preparing you for something. ***Then, seize*** that opportunity.

Moses prayed in Psalm 90:12, "So teach us to number our days, that we may apply our hearts unto wisdom." Numbering our days means evaluating the quality of our time spent. Not only must we consider where our time goes, but how we spend it and why.

We are called by God to be people of faith, to trust God, His perfect will, and His perfect time. There is a combination of time and trust. I must trust that God will elevate at the appointed and opportune time.

Ask Yourself…

- *What is God preparing me for at this time?*
- *What divine opportunity is God asking me to seek?*
- *In my kairos moments, what am I seeking…what am I focused on?*

Discipline Yourself…

To live in God's kairos moments requires focus. As servant-leader you must focus on

- *What God wants not what he or she wants.*

- *What are God ideas not just good ideas.*
- *What decisions are right for eternity…not just for now.*

List the critically important opportunities before you right now. Prioritize them based on the criteria above. Now, ask God to help you make plans to implement ways to maximize the opportunities from Him.

Chapter 3

Help! My Anointing Does Not Match My Assignment

Then Samuel took the horn of oil and anointed him in the midst of his brothers and the Spirit of the Lord came upon David from that day forward.
(1 Samuel 16:13)

At a young age, David was anointed by Samuel to be king. This must have been an exciting day. His entire family sees this crowning moment. Surely God is ready to elevate him to the throne. Surely, he is getting fitted for his royal robe. Surely, his servants are lining up to take marching orders from their new leader. Where does God send his new servant leader?

> *But David occasionally went and returned from Saul*
> *to feed his father's sheep at Bethlehem*
> (1 Samuel 17:15)

So, the anointed king is feeding his father's sheep? Although he was anointed for kingship, God has a journey of preparation. On the journey toward purpose, one must prepare for seasons when your anointing does not match your assignment. God anoints David to lead His people, but He puts him in a position to demonstrate faithfulness over the simple. Most people struggle with the feeling that they are not doing enough or doing what they were called to do. David exemplifies how to remain faithful over the seemingly insignificant and straightforward assignments. There was not a task that was too big or too small for David. For example, notice David's simple assignment and his attention to detail in this passage:

THE ASSIGNMENT

> [17] *Then Jesse said to his son David,*
> *"Take now for your brothers an ephah of this dried grain*
> *and these ten loaves and run to your brothers at the camp.*
> [18] *And carry these ten cheeses to the captain of their thousand,*
> *and see how your brothers fare, and bring back news of them."*
> 1 Samuel 17:17-18 (NKJV)

The assignment was very simple: (1) take your brothers some grain and some bread, (2) take some cheeses to the captain, (3) check on your brothers' well-being, and (4) bring me back a report. How simple is that? Too simple for an anointed king... This is not something that someone with his level of anointing should be doing. But notice David's attention to detail...

Help! My Anointing Does Not Match My Assignment

20 So David rose early in the morning, left the sheep with a keeper, and took the things and went as Jesse had commanded him....
22 And David left his supplies in the hand of the supply keeper, ran to the army, and came and greeted his brothers.
1 Samuel 17:20, 22 (NKJV)

Many people fail to notice David's attention to detail. He did not allow his anointing for his next assignment to diminish his faithfulness to his current assignment. Despite the simplicity of the assignment, David displayed faithfulness. David did not let what others said about his position minimize his efforts to please God. In *1 Samuel 17:28*, his oldest brother Eliab was angry that David showed up at the battleground and asked, "With whom did you leave those few sheep in the wilderness?" David had the maturity and the presence of mind to turn away. He was proud of his assignment and faithful to his father and would not allow distractors to discourage him. This is valuable to everyone who faces the challenges of being turned away from an opportunity because one does not possess the title or position. One must understand that God is developing his servants for future assignments.

As an Associate minister I did not become consumed with just the preaching opportunities and overlooked the simple tasks of serving. I was asked to clean up in the absence of the church custodian, lock up the building after choir rehearsal, drive the bus for a youth trip, make sure the light bulbs were working on the church marquee and change the batteries in the microphone. Whatever the tasks may be, do it to the glory of the Lord. David Hopewell, Sr. in his book, *Keys to Becoming an Effective Associate Minister and Church Leader,* suggests that many associate ministers have a problem with serving. Hopewell writes, "Some associates feel that once they have been called into ministry, then they are above serving. They do not want to gird themselves with the towel of humility, as Jesus did, and serve others."⁸

Serving is doing what needs to be done to support the vision of God in the ministry where one serves.

Although David had been anointed to be king, he was humble enough to continue his job as keeper of his father's sheep. David's humility is a critical component of his exaltation. Although he was anointed, he remained faithful to his assignment. This is consistent with *Matthew 25:21*, "Well done, good and faithful servant! You have been faithful over a few things; I will put you in charge of many things." Remember to pay attention to the details of the seemingly insignificant tasks.

The Impact of Being Faithful Over the Simple

Because of his faithfulness, David could see results that impacted the kingdom. His diligence and dedication in protecting his father's sheep from a bear and a lion, brought prosperity to his father. When asked to play the harp for Saul, the Scriptures report, "Saul would become refreshed and well, and the distressing spirit would depart from him." When he was chosen to fight Goliath, his victory enabled all the people of Israel to experience victory and peace.

Your faithfulness has an influence and impact despite your position or title.

Do you understand the impact of faithfulness to every assignment? Serving in the subordinate leader position can impact the body of Christ. Joseph was able to serve all of Egypt from the second-in-command position. One must be able to maintain a broad influence even with limited responsibilities. Faithfulness adds value to the organization. In Exodus 17, we see Aaron and Hur, simply holding up Moses' hands during the battle. It's amazing that an assignment so simple can be so significant. Most people would have loved to be Moses and Joshua, but without the faithfulness of Aaron and Hur over the simple assignment, victory could have been null and void.

Can God trust you to be faithful over the simple when your anointing does not match your assignment? David demonstrates that if you are faithful over the simple assignments, God can change your assignment in the process. As David was fulfilling his simple assignment for his father, Jesse, he met Goliath. He didn't go seeking Goliath. Nevertheless, God intervenes on the path of faithfulness to the simple assignment.

Being faithful over the simple assignments will lead to great opportunities. Therefore, one must be prepared to embrace and maximize every opportunity.

Mike Bonem and Roger Patterson in *Leading From the Second Chair* suggest that associates be prepared to recognize and act on unique moments that can shape you and set you apart. David maximized his opportunity when faced with the giant, Goliath. Defeating this giant shaped the rest of his life and set him apart from others in Saul's army. Dr. Joseph Walker III highlights this element of embracing every opportunity in his book, *No Opportunity Wasted: The Art of Execution*. Dr. Walker states, "You don't get to determine what parts of the assignment you will embrace. When you are walking in complete purpose, brace yourself for all things you expect, as well as the unexpected."[9]

Those who have been faithful over every assignment can share in the glory of God. This can be seen in Jesus' discourse with his Father in John 17. Jesus says, "I have brought you glory on earth by completing the work you gave me to do. And now, Father, glorify me in your presence with the glory I had with you before the world began. In essence, Jesus says, *I have been faithful over the tasks given to me.*

The Discipline of Simplicity

> "Three rules of work: (1) Out of clutter find simplicity. (2) From discord find harmony. (3) In the middle of difficulty lies opportunity."
> —Albert Einstein

Simplicity begins by separating the essential from the nonessential things in life. It proceeds to choose God ideas over good ideas and then focuses on what's particular over what's general. Simplicity desires only what's purposefully productive over what's overdone, overpriced, and overestimated. Simplicity requires diligence, excellence, patience, and lasting impact. David discovered the freedom of simplicity in being a servant-leader.

Ask yourself…

- *Are there any assignments that I feel are beneath my anointing?*
- *Am I being asked to do the simple assignments?*
- *Do I understand the impact of my anointing?*
- *Can I be trusted with more by displaying maturity?*
- *Will I be ready when faithfulness meets opportunity?*

Discipline Yourself…

Review the assignments you are now executing. Simplify each one so that only essential and necessary tasks are done to complete each assignment.

Chapter 4

Your Gift Will Make Room for You

A man's gift makes room for him and brings him before great men.
(Proverbs 18:16 NKJV)

So Saul said to his servants, "Provide me now a man who can play well, and bring him to me." Then one of the servants answered and said, "Look, I have seen a son of Jesse the Bethlehemite, who is skillful in playing, a mighty man of valor, a man of war, prudent in speech, and a handsome person; and the LORD is with him."
(1 Samuel 16:17-18 NKJV)

David was very skilled and talented. When Saul needed someone who could play well, his servants described this young kid who was extremely skilled. He was a warrior, a musician, and effective communicator. He was fearless in battle, faithful in service, and creative in composing music. In 1 Chronicles 25, we see King David organizing the music ensemble for the temple. He is credited for composing at least seventy-three psalms. David was what we would call "a jack of all trades." He had an impeccable resume.

When you examine his resume, he seems to be TOO GIFTED for his current responsibilities: take care of the father's sheep, take your brothers some food, and help your father in the field. He is anointed to be king, skilled beyond measure, and handsome; but he is tending sheep? If David was in the 21st century, he would need to hire a marketing or branding agent to "get him noticed." David needed to promote himself. How did he expect to get recognized in the field keeping his father's sheep?

This a danger that derails many gifted and talented leaders. They feel the urge to get noticed. They seek positions, power, prestige based on their talents. They can't comprehend why people with inferior gifts, substandard skills, and less talent are being elevated. They make the mistake of self-promoting their talent rather than trusting God's timing.

David was patient because he was a servant with skills, talents, and God-given abilities. He would rather be faithful than famous. He demonstrates that faithfulness would find opportunity. David didn't force his way into a door; God opened it. If you are patient, the opportunities of life will match your gifts and abilities. David was blessed with great talent, but God controlled the timing.

Trust God's Divine Providence

David didn't get into the palace by accident, chance, or coincidence, but by Divine Providence. Divine Providence simply means that God controls all things in the universe. Through divine providence, God accomplishes His will. His will was for David to be King of Israel. Israel had a king named Saul. How does God replace the people's king with His chosen man without putting him in danger? He arranges a situation where the king needed a musician. A door opened for a musician, not a king.

Although David was anointed to be king, it was his musical gift that introduces him into the royal court. Only God! God orchestrated a need and provided His chosen instrument to meet that need.

Israel needed a deliverer, God said, *I will send Moses.* There was a famine in the land, someone was needed to handle the famine. God said, I *will send Joseph.* The gospel needed to reach the Gentiles. God said, *I will send Paul.* This world needed a Savior. God said, I *will send my Son to seek and the save the lost.*

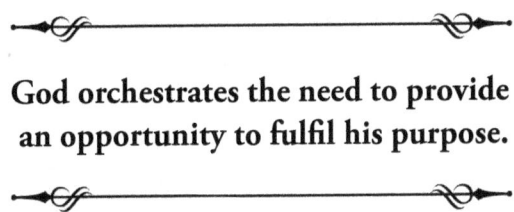

God orchestrates the need to provide an opportunity to fulfil his purpose.

Divine Providence and Human Preparation

Saul said, *"Provide me now a man who can "play well."* God's control of life circumstances does not eliminate human responsibility. David was a shepherd boy who loved music. Although he was in the field with the sheep, he still utilized his gifts and talents. Often, we allow the geographical location to place limits on the demonstration of our gifts and talents. I hear people say, *if only I was on the stage; I would sing just like them. If only I was in the spotlight, I would shine like them.*

Gifts are given to be displayed regardless of the location. David was using his skills in his service. He was exercising his gift because he knew it was God-given. Psalm 139:13-14 reveals, "For you created my inmost being; you knit me together in my mother's womb. I praise you because I am fearfully and wonderfully made; your works are wonderful; I know that full well (NIV)."

God knows where you are. You do not have to seek fame, fortune, or opportunities. You must trust in the Sovereignty of God. The same God who gives the talents handles the timing. The same God who provides the skills sent the servants to hear David's music. David praised God in the fields and some anonymous servants recognized his gifts. One of the Saul's servants said, "I know somebody." Not all the servants. Just one of the servants.

When you are part of God's will, you don't need everyone to notice you, just the right person. David was faithful in serving not being seen. But because he was serving, God arranged for him to be seen.

Evidently, David left a strong impression on the servant. We are not informed on when or where he saw David, but we do know that whenever or wherever the servant saw David, he remembered him!

This is similar to Joseph in prison. He met a cupbearer in prison and displayed his gifts in prison. In prison, he demonstrated his God-given abilities. Although he did not deserve to be in prison, the prison did not limit his loyalty to God. Like David, his gift was noticed outside of a place of prominence. Two years later, God orchestrates a situation where Joseph's gift is needed in the palace. Once again, God's servant does not have to seek position. His gift will make room for him and bring him before a leader who needs his service.

Your Gift Provides Entrance And Elevation

God orchestrates an opportunity for David's musical talents to gain him entrance into the royal court. God was not only orchestrating his entrance, but also his exaltation. 1 Samuel 16:21 reads, "David came to Saul and **entered his service**. Saul liked him very much, and David became one of his armor-bearers." The armor bearer's function is to protect his master's honor. This is a position that commanded extreme loyalty. He was needed to provide protection for the king. David was a keeper of his father's sheep. He was trained in providing protection.

Remember the servant described David as a "mighty man of valor and a man of war." He had not served in an army. He developed a reputation in the field. This seemingly insignificant role in his life would provide another opportunity for God to enlarge his territory.

David is now in the palace. He is a new position, not yet fulfilling his purpose… But God's plan is still in progress. Let's keep track…a musician is needed…David is skilled in that. Then, Goliath shows up and a warrior is needed…David is skilled in that also. God continues to arrange situations that require David's skillset.

One day, "A WARRIOR" was needed to protect and defend God's people. What was David doing? Protecting and defending his father's sheep. There is a correlation. God was preparing David with this assignment for his next assignment. David was qualified for Saul's army. However, he was sent to his father's field. Often, God trains you in private before elevating you publicly.

EXPERIENCE NEEDED!

When David shows up on the scene, he was only there to give his brothers some food (1 Samuel 17:17). He did not go looking for war, but God had equipped him for battle. God does not wait until war to equip His servants. We are already prepared for battle. David had the anointing and the ability, but not the age. Saul said to him, you are not able to defeat this warrior, you are only a youth…." I love David's response. Paraphrasing what he said, "You don't know my history or my destiny. God gave me a season of preparation in the field, for such a time as this."

> *34 But David said to Saul, "Your servant has been keeping his father's sheep. When a lion or a bear came and carried off a sheep from the flock, 35 I went after it, struck it and rescued the sheep from its mouth. When it turned on me, I seized it by its hair, struck it and killed it. 36 Your servant has killed both the lion and the bear; this uncircumcised Philistine will be like one of them, because he has defied the armies of the living God. 37 The LORD who delivered me from the paw of the lion and the paw of the bear will deliver me from the hand of this Philistine." Saul said to David, "Go, and the LORD be with you."*
> (1 Samuel 17:34-37 NIV)

David was able to display his skills, abilities, and talents in the valley on that day, because his skills and abilities were developed in the fields with his father's sheep. Although he had the ability, God developed a confident attitude in him. He was confident that God would give him victory. That confidence was developed long before it was needed on history's stage. It was developed behind the scenes.

Beforehand and behind the scenes, God began to develop David's character, integrity, and loyalty. It was in the fields that

God developed his leadership skills as a shepherd. While in the fields tending his father's sheep, David was utilizing his skills as a shepherd. Although David was gifted in many areas, God developed him into the leader He desired. This is God's plan and God's way.

GOD USES *EXPERIENCES* TO SHAPE, MOLD, AND DEVELOP OUR GIFTS FOR THE JOURNEY AHEAD.

Leadership is not dependent on gifts, talents, and abilities alone. Giftedness alone does not produce results in ministry. Many gifted and talented ministers have not allowed their gifts to be developed. David was maturing and getting valuable experience while God was orchestrating the affairs of his life. In the remarkable book, *Shepherd Leadership: Wisdom for Leaders from Psalm 23*, leadership experts Blaine McCormick and David Davenport introduce a new kind of leader by offering a new image of leadership— the leader as a shepherd.

David was trained as a shepherd boy. This training enabled him to become the shepherd of the flock of Israel. What he learned in private was later manifested on the throne. What you learn in private with God will be displayed in public. Associate ministers must be mindful of God's private plan of development. There are some valuable lessons in the wilderness that cannot be learned in the limelight.

Dave Earley writes, "Often we mistake what qualifies us to minister effectively to others. Gifts are important, but we often overlook the fact that it is in the loneliness of the wilderness and the difficulties of the desert that God truly prepares us to minister to others. God uses wilderness for training ground; it is there that God teaches dependence, trust, and obedience."

Everyone has a gift that needs to be developed and displayed. God has put a unique gift in each of us that will enable us to fulfil our purpose.

- *Are you maximizing your gift for the glory of God?*
- *Are you waiting until you get the position to utilize your gifts?*

God blessed David with a variety of gifts to serve in the kingdom. His gifts brought him before the right people at the right time for the right purpose. Romans 12:6 says, "Having then gifts differing according to the grace that is given to us, let us use them."

Ask Yourself…

- *Are you promoting your gift or preparing for your opportunity?*
- *God entrusted you with talent, can you trust him with timing?*
- *Are you operating with the goal to be noticed?*

Remember This… God Knows Where You Are!

Discipline Yourself…

As God prepares you with a variety of experiences to develop your skills and gifts, will you stay in the moment, discipline yourself, and strive for excellence in all that God has you learning?

Chapter 5

WHY AM I HERE?

*1 David left Gath and escaped to the cave of Adullum.
When his brothers and his father's household heard about it,
they went down to him there.
2 All those who were in distress or in debt or discontented gathered
around him, and he became their leader.
About four hundred men were with him.*
(1 Samuel 22:1-2 NIV)

In 1958, the Federal Highway Act was passed. That act says Rest Areas are to be provided on Interstate highways as a safety measure. Safety rest areas provide motorists with off-road spaces for emergency stopping and resting for short periods. For more than half a century, old-fashioned, basic highway rest stops have welcomed motorists looking for a break from the road. They were not designed for long-term lodging just temporary relief from the journey. Rest stops are one of the many tools to keep motorists safe and help them arrive at their destination alive.

Highway rest areas are critical for truck drivers' safety and their ability to comply with a federal law limiting the number of hours they can drive without rest. Just like the Highway Safety Commission, God also knows that his servants get weary along the journey. We need a place where we can refresh, get relief, get renewed, and get restored. This place may not be a place of desire, but it is necessary.

Every servant that God uses has a peculiar place that is necessary for growth and development. For Joseph, it was a prison. For Moses, it was in Pharoah's home and the backside of the wilderness. For Elijah, God sent him to a brook where he learned to trust in God's provision. For Paul, it was Arabia. *Have you spent time in your necessary place?*

David's necessary place was the cave of Addulum. David knew that he was anointed to be king, but he was not assigned to the position. He had the power of the Lord without the position. On the journey to the position, God had prepared a place for him to become what he was called to be. It was in the cave that he BECAME their leader. Saul was the king, but in the cave, David became their leader. After careful examination, I discovered that God uses the necessary place for various reasons. In this chapter we will discover some of those reasons.

"David left Gath and escaped to the cave of Adullum"

GOD USES THE NECESSARY PLACE TO
FULFILL THE NECESSARY PURPOSE

The text uses an interesting word for David's arrival to this place. It says that he "escaped" to the cave. The text did not say that he came to the cave or arrived at a cave. It says that he escaped to the cave. This suggests that he was in the midst of imminent and impending danger. In the midst of danger, God uses "this place" as a place of deliverance. God knows when you need relief. God knows when you need refuge. He provides David this place of escape called *Addulum*. The word Addulum means "refuge." So many times, we fail to understand why God has us in certain places and predicaments for periods of time. At the time he couldn't go to his home, couldn't go to Jonathan, couldn't go to the temple, nor could he go to Samuel. He needed a place of safety and God provided a "refuge."

David was in the cave but he didn't give the cave credit for being his refuge. Psalm 46:1 reads, "God is our refuge and strength, a very present help in trouble." Psalm 27:5, "For in a time of trouble, he shall hide me". Although Addulum served in a physical capacity to provide protection from Saul, David realized that God had him in that place. God was behind this place for a purpose. David needed the cave to hide from Saul. He also needed the cave to hide from self. In the previous chapter, David began to compromise his integrity and attempt to fit in among the enemy. So, David not only needed a place of refuge from Saul, but also from himself.

Songwriter Bruce Parham says, "Oh hide me from circumstances; hide me, when I want to take one more chance, I need you to Hide me when my strength is weak, hide me when my eyes want to take one more glance, Oh hide me, Lord I need you to hide me, hide me from the enemy, Oh hide me, I need you to hide me, Lord I'm asking you to hide me, Even if the enemy you hide is me." On this journey toward our destiny, God may need to provide safety from self. If we are not careful, self-destruction will be our greatest enemy.

It is interesting when you read this story, David is on the verge of coming apart mentally. He begins to hide out in Goliath's home territory. He pretends to be crazy so that the people don't kill him. He nearly lost his mind, his morals, and his wellbeing. David is acting foolishly, feeling frustrated, and seemed forsaken. The cave now became a place of restoration.

It has been stated that athletes need sufficient days of rest for their muscles to grow and develop. They take their bodies through rigorous training to achieve their desired results. Most trainers will tell you that to effectively achieve this goal, the muscles need a period of rest. So does the servant of God. God uses pain, suffering, persecution, trials, tests, and adverse circumstances to mature and develop us. Through this rough period, David has spent time talking with his best friend Jonathan. He begged the priest in Nob to give him a weapon. He tries to blend in with the enemy. While in the cave, David now communicated with God.

In the cave he wrote Psalm 142. In this Psalm, he cried out to God. He poured out his complaint. He let God know that he was overwhelmed, lonely, and frustrated. It was in the cave where he reconnected with God. It was in the cave where he refocused on his mission. It was in the cave where he learned how to lean and depend on God. In the cave he regained his composure, his confidence; his strength; and his sanity. The cave was a place of refuge and a place of restoration.

God Uses the Necessary Place to Connect You To Necessary People

David had an opportunity to reconnect with God. God then sent him some complicated company. God sent those in debt, those in need, and those who were discontent. This company was seemingly useless, worthless, and insignificant. Although David was experiencing personal adversity, he shows us that trouble does not give us a license to focus exclusively on ourselves.

God did not send him the people he desired. God sent him the ones who were required. God sent company that helped his growth and development. These men came to David when he was down and out. They came to David when he didn't have anything but a promise and potential. God will put you in seasonal situations that allow you to see the real and relevant people you need to help shape your character. God sent some guys that David could trust. They were with David when he didn't have anything. That's when you know you have a friend. Proverbs 17:17, "A friend loves at all times, and a brother is born for adversity."

Once David arrived at the throne, he would be surrounded by a crowd of people, but he could tell who was committed in the cave. God sent him a group of people he could trust and train. The scripture says, *"He became their captain."* These men believed in David and David poured into them. These men believed in David and David invested in them. David was anointed "To Be King" in 1 Samuel 16. But in the cave, "HE BECAME." God will develop you in private. God will mold you, mend you, and model you in private. By God's Spirit, "we are becoming like Christ, in his death" (Philippians 3:10 NIV). *In the cave, David's self was being crucified and was becoming the character God needed in a king.* (Read Philippians 2)

GOD USES PLACES FOR PURPOSE ~
THESE PLACES ARE NECESSARY NOT PERMANENT

So many times, we get involved in trying to build our own lives, careers, and fail to understand that God has a bigger plan and purpose for our lives. The cave of Addulum was a place where David could stop and see the plan that God had for his life. He could have easily got distracted by Saul and his antics. He could have easily gotten frustrated because he was anointed but not on the throne. He understood that God was at work.

You may be asking yourself; how long do I have to stay in this situation, how long do I have to deal with these people or how long do I have to keep suffering in this situation. The answer is simple: "Until You Know."

David was reminded by the prophet that the cave was temporary. Gad said to David, use the cave for instruction. Use the cave for refuge. Use the cave for reconciliation. Just don't stay in the cave! Your destination is not in the cave. The cave is just a temporary lay-over not your final destination.

If you are discouraged in your cave, understand that where you are right now is not where you shall be. It is the *kairos* moment God appointed for a season.

GOD USES THE NECESSARY PLACE FOR A PLACE OF PRAYER AND PRAISE

The cave of Addulum turned into a great prayer closet. God often puts us in peculiar and painful places to push us to pray.

- *Jonah in the fish ~ from inside the belly of the fish, Jonah called on the Lord in his distress*

- *Jesus in the garden of Gethsemane ~ in the garden, He cried out, Father if it possible remove this cup*

- *Jacob at Bethel ~ at that place Jacob wrestled all night and said, I will not let you go until you bless me*

- *Paul and Silas in Prison ~ in prison they prayed and sang songs and God delivered them*

When you study the Psalms written inside the cave, you notice David shifting from prayer to praise. In Psalm 142, we find David on his face before God, "I cry aloud to the LORD; I lift up my voice to the LORD for mercy, I pour out my complaint before him; before him I tell my trouble. I cry to you, O LORD; I say, 'You are my refuge, my portion in the land of the living.'" Listen to my cry, for I am in desperate need; rescue me from those who pursue me, for they are too strong for me (vs 1,2,5,6). He gained confidence after calling on the name of the Lord. In Psalm 57, the psalmist pens, "Have mercy on me, O God, have mercy on me, for in you my soul takes refuge. I will take refuge in the shadow of your wings until the disaster has passed. My heart is steadfast, O God, my heart is steadfast; I will sing and make music (vs. 1,7). The psalmist seems to move from his face to his knees. He is displaying courage and confidence in the God of his salvation.

Finally, he pens Psalm 34, "I will bless the LORD at all times; His praise shall continually be in my mouth. My soul shall make its boast in the LORD; The humble shall hear of it and be glad. Oh, magnify the LORD with me, and let us exalt His name together" (vs. 1-3). David is extoling the Lord. He encourages those who are discontented, discouraged, and defeated to join in the praise. The cave served its purpose.

When I study this time in David's life, I am reminded of one of my favorite songs by Andre Crouch. Andre Crouch had gone through some trials and tribulations in his life. In those most difficult days, he discovered some things about God. He penned the song, *Through It All*. Remember this line, "…in every situation, God gave me blessed consolation, that my trials come to only make me strong."

Ask Yourself…

- *Has God positioned you in your necessary place?*
- *"Why am I here?" and "What I can learn while I am here?"*
- *What did you learn about leaning on and depending on God?*

Discipline Yourself…

When you find yourself in a cave, journal your prayer life…

_____

_____

_____

Chapter 6

PLEASE BE PATIENT WITH ME... GOD IS AT WORK

Wait on the Lord; Be of good courage,
And He shall strengthen your heart; Wait, I say, on the Lord!
(Psalm 27:14)

Many people can define patience, but they struggle to demonstrate and apply it. Patience, at its best, is the ability to remain calm and tranquil while waiting for something to happen. It's the mental and emotional ability to accept that some things take time. Patience reveals our faith in God's timing, God's omnipotence, and God's loyal love. Let's be clear; waiting on God is difficult. God trains His leaders by going through a process of development that requires patience.

As David reflected on his journey to becoming king, he acknowledged the need for patience as God worked on his behalf.

David waited more than thirteen years to take the throne after the prophet Samuel anointed him to be the next king. Thirteen years of crucial training between the choosing and the coronation. God could have taken him straight to the throne, but David wasn't ready. God does not measure spiritual growth in minutes, months, or years. He measures the growth of one's character as that character is conformed to the image of Christ—a Shepherd and a Servant.

During those years of training, David faithfully took care of his father's sheep. It might have seemed like a menial position, but he knew he had bigger things inside of him. He had heard the prophet say that he was a king, but he had to pass the test in the waiting room before elevation to the throne. He had to show God he would take care of his father's sheep before God would trust him to take care of His people. There was a process of evaluation before elevation.

God is never in a hurry. He told Noah to build a boat because of the coming flood. The flood didn't come until 120 years later. God promised Abraham and Sarah a child, but they waited 25 years. Isaac and Rebekah waited 20 years for their child. The Israelites waited 440 years before entering the Promised Land. Jacob waited 14 years before marrying the wife of choice. Are you willing to wait on the Lord? Is it worth the wait?

When one reads the Psalms, there is evidence of David's patience being developed. Have you ever noticed how many of the Psalms are written during times of waiting? The question, "how long...?" is found fairly frequently in the Psalms, as is, "wait on the Lord." David understood that God had a plan and a purpose for his life. David's responsibility was to remain patient in the process. As we examine the Psalms of David, there are some key principles that will aid us in our battle to persevere.

Careful study of scriptures seems to suggest the term "WAITING ON GOD", originates with David. The term is used at least twenty-five times. There were others before David who waited, but it seems like they were waiting on something else. David was waiting ON GOD.

Abraham was waiting on a son…

Moses was waiting on Pharoah to change his mind…

Joseph was waiting on his position…

David makes it clear that he was waiting on God.

PATIENCE REQUIRES TRUST IN GOD

To experience fulfillment while waiting on God, one must have trust in God. What does TRUST mean? It is absolutely the highest level of a confidence in something or someone. When you have absolute trust in the Lord there are no other alternatives. Throughout the Psalms, David reveals his supreme confidence in God, regardless of the circumstances and situations.

In Psalm 13, David asks the question: *How long?*

- *How long will you forget me?*
- *How long will you hide your face from me?*
- *How long must I take counsel in my soul and have sorrow in my heart?*

The pressure of waiting is causing him to cry out to God. David is feeling afraid and abandoned. He feels abandoned by friends, family and even God. It is in this time of testing, that David reveals why God calls him "a man after his own heart." David is honest about his circumstances. He is feeling the pain of waiting on God's deliverance. His pain causes him to pray to the God he is waiting on. The pain pushes him to a powerful place: a place of prayer. What a prescription! In vs. 5, David concludes, "But I trust in your unfailing love…" David is saying "I feel abandoned. I feel alone. I feel afraid. I feel anxious. But, I trust in You." Why does David put his trust in God? In the midst of the pain, pressure, and agony, David is reminded of "God's resume" He concludes in verse 6, **"for he [God] has been good to me."**

While you wait, recall "God's resume." While you wait, recall God's past performances. So, David concludes, I will continue to trust God's plan, God's purpose, God's process, and God's protection.

When waiting on God, many people put their trust in their schemes, plans, and resources. God will place us in situations where we must lean on Him and Him alone. David says in Psalm 20:7, "Some trust in chariots and some in horses, but we trust in the name of the Lord our God". This is valuable for those who are waiting on God. There will be the temptation to consider alternatives to find fulfillment.

As an associate minister I recall a friend telling me he knew the chairman of the search committee at a vacant church. He knew my frustration in my current position, and he knew that I was determined to wait on God. Yet, he gave me the person's number to call and set up a meeting. After a few weeks, the guy called me and said he was given my number and asked if I was looking for a fresh start or new assignment. I told him *yes*, I was awaiting on my next assignment, but God was working on planting me in my place of purpose. He said, "Yes that's good, but what Sunday can you come and talk with our committee?"

I laughed and said, "Sir, I have not heard from God about becoming a candidate of any vacant churches at the moment. Thanks for the consideration and the invitation." Like David, I was putting my trust in God.

If you feel you are stuck in God's waiting room, reject impatience, and put your trust in God. God knows who you are and where you are. God knows the place He has for you. Don't be weary in well doing and trust that God's timing is perfect.[10]

Proverbs 3:5-6 declares, "Trust in the Lord with all your heart, And lean not on your own understanding; In all your ways acknowledge Him, And He shall direct your paths".

Your Expectations Helps You Handle What You Are Experiencing

David expected God to deliver him every time because he developed trust in God. Not sometime, but every time. Although David recognized the challenges from his enemies, he remained confident. David expected God to keep him and keep his promises. In Psalm 27:14, notice that David had confidence in the Lord that God would hold him, keep him, and deliver him. David trusted in the Lord that he would see His goodness. That special confidence he had in God sustained him.

The word "patience" carries with it an expectation of a result. David was confident that waiting on God would yield profitable results. In Psalm 40, some of the results include:

1) God inclined to me and heard my cry,

2) *God also brought me up out of a horrible pit, out of the miry clay,*

3) *The Lord set my feet upon a rock,*

4) *God established my steps, and*

5) *The Lord put a new song in my mouth.*

In Psalm 37, those who wait shall inherit the land. The question becomes how can David be so confident in these results? In Psalm 25 we find the answer:

God is Faithful vs. 3

God's Word is Truth vs. 4 and 5

God is Savior vs. 5

God is Merciful and Loving vs. 6

God is Good and Upright vs. 8

God is Loving and Faithful in All His Ways vs. 10

God is Forgiving vs. 11

God is Gracious vs. 16

God is Powerful and Provides Refuge vs. 20

In 1 Samuel 16, David was anointed to be king. Although God was taking him through a season of testing, he kept his expectation that God would fulfil His promise. Many people struggle with patience because they have lost their expectation. Are you expecting God to do what he said in His Word?

David expected to be king, even when his expectations didn't match his current experiences. When he faced the bear and the lion, he knew he would be victorious, because he was expecting to become king. When he faced Goliath, he knew he would be victorious because he was expecting to become king. When he was feeding and caring for his father's sheep, he didn't get weary in well doing, because he was expecting to become king. When he was running for his life, he knew he would survive, because he was expecting to become king. He did not know all the details, but he trusted God with his destination.

In 1 Kings 18:41-45, Elijah was expecting rain, because God had promised rain. His expectation was connected to God's promise. He understood that if God promised, it would come to pass. Despite the drought. Despite the famine. Elijah waited patiently on the Lord. One day, he got word from his servant, "There is a cloud, as small as a man's hand, rising out of the sea!" That was all Elijah needed to hear. He began to prepare for what he was expecting.

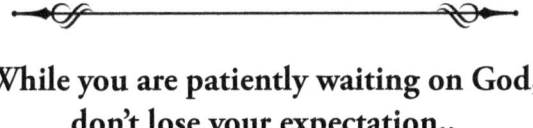

While you are patiently waiting on God, don't lose your expectation..

While You Wait, Keep Serving

Patience is not about inactivity. While David was waiting on God, he did not passively sit around pouting and complaining. Waiting by itself, accomplishes nothing. *There is a thin line between patience and procrastination.* David found fulfilment in serving others, whether it was keeping his father's sheep, playing the harp for Saul, looking after his brothers, or leading Israel in battle. When you find that sense of contentment in your heart, knowing that you are in God's will, then you are free to serve with sincerity while you wait. Strive to put aside your own agenda and seek to follow God's plan as you serve where you are planted.

There was no shame in waiting on God. Although some may have laughed at him because they knew he was anointed to be next; he understood those who wait on God will not be put to shame. In Psalm 25:3, David tells us what he learned about patiently waiting for God, "Surely none who wait for You will be put to shame; but those who are faithless without cause will be disgraced." The last part of this verse is a clear warning for us not try and get ahead of God's timing or to get impatient as we wait until God says we are ready to move to the next level. David was basically saying, "God, my time is in Your hands. I not only trust Your ways, but I trust Your timing. I know at the right time, when I'm ready, when I can handle it, you will shift me to my next level."

In my research for my doctoral dissertation, I learned that 40 percent of all associate ministers described themselves as impatient. They knew they did not have the patience to wait. The 40 percent also revealed they had submitted a resume to another church for another assignment. This lack of patience has caused several associate ministers to move ahead of God's plan and purpose. Their desire to lead and serve as a pastor forced them to develop a sense of frustration with their pastor. They were not allowed to operate on their own terms.

We must understand that God measures patience with maturity not movement. Some people feel because they are active and constantly moving, they are making an impact on the kingdom. Sometimes maturity does not come with activity. Maturity is developed in stillness. In Psalm 37:7, David reminds us, "Be still before the LORD and wait patiently for Him...."

WHILE YOU WAIT, BE PREPARED FOR TEMPTATION

While you wait, know that you will be tempted to become impatient. Impatience occurs when we doubt the wisdom of God's timing or the goodness of his direction. In the season of waiting, we must guard the temptation to take matters into your own hands or run ahead of God. Impatience is risky and more than likely will result in disappointment and even disaster. Don't feel discouraged if you are fighting this battle. Many believers have lost the battle of impatience. Scripture offers plenty of examples of saints who got weary of waiting for God and chose to do things their way. Abraham and Sarah took matters into their own hands and had to deal with Hagar. The children of Israel took matters into their own hands while awaiting Moses and built a golden calf. Saul, Israel's first king, refused to wait on Samuel and his impatience cost him dearly.

WHILE YOU WAIT…MONITOR WHAT YOU HEAR?

Psalm 11, David's friends, family, or counsel were telling him to flee. He responds, "In the Lord I put my trust; How can you say to my soul, "Flee as a bird to your mountain?" David was determined to stand on his solid foundation. Although they may have had his best interest at heart, God controlled his destiny. David put his trust in God.

In 1 Samuel 24, David and his men were in a cave and Saul was there relieving himself in the same cave. David's men whispered to him, "Now is your opportunity! Today the lord is telling you, I will certainly put your enemy into your power, to do as you wish." For an instance, David almost yielded to the temptation. It was an opportunity, but it was not God's Divine Opportunity. 1 Samuel 24:5 reports, "But then David's conscience began bothering him because he had cut Saul's robe." David was so in tune with God that, in the battle of impatience, he surrendered to the will and ways of God. In the season of waiting, one must monitor the voices that feed our faith or fuel our frustrations.

WHILE YOUR WAIT.... MONITOR WHAT YOU SEE?

As we wait on God, He orchestrates divine appointments that strengthen our faith in the process. With this in mind, we must be watching, while we wait. In Luke 8, Jairus was on the journey with Jesus to receive healing for his daughter at home. Suddenly, they went from walking mode to waiting mode. While he was in wait mode, God gave him something to witness. A woman with an issue of blood pressed her way through the crowd and received supernatural healing. Jesus demanded her to tell her story. He proclaimed; her faith has made her well. Jairus witnessed a woman be delivered from a 12-year blood flow. He was a witness to the healing power of Jesus Christ.

While in wait mode, he was given a courtside view of the Lord's power. A few minutes later, Luke records, "While he was still speaking to her, a messenger arrived from the home of Jairus, the leader of the synagogue. He told him, 'Your daughter is dead. There is no use troubling the Teacher now'" (Luke 8:49). Jairus was given visible evidence to overcome what he just heard. David said, "I would have fainted, unless I had believed that I would see the goodness of the Lord in the land of the living" Psalm 27:13. Keep watching while you wait.

MONITOR HOW YOU FEEL

While you wait, monitor what you are feeling. If you are not careful, your feelings will cause you to make fleshly decisions.

When reading the Psalms, there were times when David was afraid, anxious, and angry. There were times when he felt abandoned by God. There were times when he felt discouraged, defeated, dejected, and dismayed. Yet, he continued to put his trust in God. In Psalm 56:3, David says, "When I am afraid, I put my trust in you." In Psalms 42:11, David speaks to his emotional soul, "Why are you cast down, O my soul? And why are you disquieted within me? Hope in God; For I shall yet praise Him, The help of my countenance and my God." While in waiting season, David continued to monitor his emotions. Overcoming his emotions enabled him to endure the process of preparation.

John the Baptist shows us that you can began to seek other solutions when emotions become overwhelming. While in prison, John was not satisfied with waiting on his deliverance. In Matthew 11, John the Baptist sends a message to Jesus, "Are you the one or should I look for another." Like many of us, John was tired of hearing about everyone else getting their breakthrough. He was sick of hearing about others being healed and delivered. He began to wonder, have you forgotten about me?

In the battle with impatience, there is the temptation to seek other solutions that will not satisfy. Jesus' response to John's disciples, "go tell John what you see and hear." While you are in waiting season, God provides sufficient evidence that He is more than worth the wait.

How To Overcome the Temptation of Impatience

Jesus gives us an example of how to deal with the temptation of impatience. God had given Jesus a specific assignment. Satan tempted Jesus to take the fast-track to fulfilling this assignment. He says something like this to Jesus, "If you really are the Son of

God then why wait on Calvary? Why take so long teaching and training? What's the purpose of going to the cross? I'll give it to you now with no cross." Jesus' ammunition to defeat the temptation of impatience was the Word of God. He continued to say, "It Is Written". We can overcome the temptation of impatience by relying on God's Word.

Patience Is Fruit That Must Be Cultivated

Patience is one of the fruits of the spirit (Galatians 5:22-23) that can be difficult for believers. Like all the other aspects of the fruit of the Spirit, patience is yet another barometer of our relationship with God. This fruit must be cultivated. David was blessed by God with incredible gifts, abilities, and talents. These abilities and talents were readily available for service, even before the anointing. The fruit of patience had to be developed.

As James suggests, patience is cultivated and developed through trials and testing (James 1:2-4). Patience is produced by responding rightly, God's way, to problems. David had his share of tests and trials while in training. During trials and troubles, he kept trusting God while being cultivated for the crowning. It takes time to cultivate this fruit. God does not measure spiritual growth and development in minutes, months, or years. He trains and develops His servants by going with a process that produces spiritual fruit. When we learn to fully trust in God, patience may not necessarily get easier, but our relationship with the Father will grow stronger.

> "Be careful about rushing God's timing. You never know who or what He is protecting you or saving you from."
> —Unknown.

**Patience gets us out of the way
and allows God to move as He desires.**

"Patience is the companion of wisdom."
– St. Augustine[11]

"The strength of Patience hangs on our capacity to believe that God is up to something good for us in all our delays and detours"[12]

"Patience is the calm acceptance that things can happen in a different order than the one you have in your mind."
David G. Allen[13]

Ministry obeys God's will, in God's Word, in God's way, and in God's timing for God's glory.

*"There is a way that seems right to a man,
but its end is the way of death."*
(Proverbs 14:12)

"Every time you wait patiently on God, it is a sign of faith and humility."
—Pastor Rick Warren

Ask Yourself…

- *Am I truly waiting patiently for God to direct my path or have I been trying to do things my way?*

Discipline Yourself…

"Position and promotion follow and never precede perspiration, perseverance, persecution, and patience. Let all those who desire promotion and position go into politics or a corporate structure. Let all those whose desire is ministry put themselves on the Potter's wheel and become willing to be shaped by perspiration, perseverance, persecution, and patience. After finishing strong, the minister will hear: 'Well done, good and faithful servant'
(Matthew 25:23)."[14]

God's Waiting Room
By Deborah Ann Belka

In God's waiting room . . .
I sometimes have to stay
at first I don't understand
the reasons for His delay
But ~ while I am in there,
it becomes obvious to me
and He shows me why
I have to wait and see.
He wants me to learn,
how to depend just on Him
and my pride and conceit
He has to pare and trim
He uses this waiting time,
for me to focus on His face
so that I can experience
the full measure of His grace.
He wants my every thought,
to be centered on His peace
though He takes His time
His love for me doesn't cease.
He wants me to understand,
that waiting has its due season
and soon I will gather and reap
the answers to His reason.
In God's waiting room . . .
I've learned about delay
and now I understand
how to trust Him every day!
Psalm 27:14

Chapter 7

Handling Applause and Adversity ~ The Price of Popularity

So David went out wherever Saul sent him and behaved wisely. And Saul set him over the men of war, and he was accepted in the sight of all the people and also in the sight of Saul's servants.... And so it was, whenever they went out, that David behaved more wisely than all the servants of Saul, so that his name became highly esteemed.
(1 Samuel 18:5-7, 30)

The writer of Ecclesiastes says that for everything, there is a season. David goes from being a "nobody in the field" to a hero overnight. He was anointed to be the next king in 1 Samuel 16. In chapter 17 he finds himself face to face with a 9-foot giant named Goliath. With God's favor, David kills Goliath and becomes "the people's champ." He is now "THE MAN." He is now walking into a season of success that he has never experienced. Is David prepared for this reality? How will people respond to this success?

> *⁶ Now it had happened as they were coming home, when David was returning from the slaughter of the Philistine, that the women had come out of all the cities of Israel, singing and dancing, to meet King Saul, with tambourines, with joy, and with musical instruments. ⁷ So the women sang as they danced, and said: "Saul has slain his thousands, And David his ten thousands."*
> (1 Samuel 18:6-7)

David's victories have brought about popularity and praise from the people. The women begin to sing praises to David. They are celebrating his success. They honored his heroics. They admired his accomplishments. David had become their hero. In 1 Samuel 18:16, *"All Israel and Judah loved David, because he went out and came in before them"*. Not only were the women singing and celebrating, but all of Israel and Judah loved David. His accomplishments were bringing about a great deal of admiration, appreciation, and applause. All of us love the applause! Applause must be handled as well as adversity. We must realize that often we are tested by the praise of people more than the problems we face.

Notice the two reactions to the applause. The applause leads to adversity and animosity between David and Saul. Saul becomes very angry and annoyed by the reaction of the people. Animosity began to set in, and he began to eye David, envy David, and scheme against David from that day forward. The applause from the people threatened the authority that he treasured in his heart. Saul understood that he was the "people's choice", but now they were cheering for another person. David faced animosity and applause. Are you willing to pay the price of popularity?

David did not allow early success to influence his behavior. He maintained his integrity and loyalty toward his superior. There is a challenge to handling the applause of people and remaining faithful to the assignment of God. David provides a model on how to handle success in a manner that pleases God.

David's name became very famous because of his success, but Scripture records that "he behaved himself wisely" *(1 Samuel 18:5,14, 30)*. This phrase is mentioned three times during 1 Samuel 18. If Scripture repeats itself, it must be important. The phrase speaks of his walk before God and man. This phrase speaks of a person who knows how to conduct themselves and walk properly. It has the idea of walking worthily and carefully.

This is extremely significant. David did not allow the success he experienced as a servant to cause him to lose focus on the task at hand. Serving faithfully was David's focus. Despite his victories, he did not allow the success to go to his head. David understood that God was the orchestrator of his destiny. Therefore, neither applause nor anger detered him from his assignment. He demonstrates that success is the byproduct of faithful service to one's purpose. Leaders must learn to not only guard against adversity and friction, but also guard against applause from early success.

How Did He Behave Himself Wisely?

1) Prioritize Purpose

God planned all that we were born to be and accomplish. Many people waste opportunities because they do not understand their purpose. God had a unique purpose for David's life.

The Prophet Samuel says, "the Lord has sought out a man after his own heart and appointed him leader of his people..." God had a plan and path for David's life beforehand. He had set him apart to lead his people. Why is understanding purpose so important? Purpose keeps us focused on the task at hand. David knew that God controlled his destiny, and he would manifest his promise in due time. So, while he waited on God, he continued to serve Saul and the people of God.

David found fulfillment in serving. Success and applause did not hinder him from serving. Saul set him over the men of war. He found success by defeating Israel's enemies. Saul needed a musician to play the harp. He found success by soothing Saul's evil spirit. Saul made him captain over a thousand. David found success by defeating the Philistines. Although David was anointed to be king, he found success in every assignment. He did not allow success to become a detriment to his destination. When he had a job to do, he did it well! He understood Colossians 3:23, "Whatever you do, do your work heartily, as for the Lord and not for people."

David was willing the serve sincerely whenever or wherever the opportunity presented itself. David was faithful in the field with no audience and faithful on the battlefield with an army of witnesses. Serving with purpose does not require a public platform. Do you need an audience to serve with sincerity?

When you prioritize purpose, you serve "in spite of" not "because of". David could have stopped serving because of the animosity he was receiving from Saul. Saul was plotting and planning to kill him with the spear. David could have stopped serving because he did not have the position. Although he was anointed by God, Saul was still king. Although the people were praising

David, Saul was still king. Despite the plots, plans, and persecution, David served faithfully and diligently... IN SPITE OF.

- In spite of the animosity, you must priority your purpose.
- In spite of the attacks, you must prioritize your purpose.

While in a Roman prison, the Apostle Paul continued to serve faithfully by maintaining the perspective that God's plans have a purpose that is greater than our pain. Listen to his perspective in Philippians 1, "Now I want you to know, brothers, that my circumstances have served to advance the gospel. As a result, it has become clear throughout the whole palace guards and to everyone else that I am in chains for Christ. And most of the brothers, confident in the Lord by my chains, now dare more greatly to speak the word without fear." My paraphrase of this would be, "Although my circumstances are not ideal, I see the impact of staying faithful to the purpose. It is possible that God will place us in circumstances that are undesirable and unwanted, that serve a greater purpose." Your situation may not be pleasurable, but it serves a purpose in God's plans for you. Knowing this, behave wisely.

This can also be seen in the life of Jesus Christ. From the beginning, Jesus knew His purpose was to die on the cross to save mankind. So, when they needed a miracle at a wedding in Cana of Galilee, He responded by saying, "What does that have to do with me? My hour has not yet come." He understood and prioritized his purpose. In John 6:15, they were ready to force Him to be their king, but He slipped away into the hills by Himself. He understood and prioritized His purpose. I did not come so that you can make me king. He was already a king fulfilling His divine purpose.

WHAT YOU BELIEVE AFFECTS HOW YOU BEHAVE

David believed God's purpose. David believed God's plan. David believed God's promise. David believed in God's protection. David believed in God's provisions. Therefore, because of what he believed, he behaved wisely. What does this mean?

When Saul was trying to kill David, he believed that God was his refuge and strength, a very present help in a time of trouble. He could have become bitter and revengeful. Yet, he believed that the Lord was with him as he walked through the valley. He believed that the Lord was his fortress and would provide the necessary protection. Because David believed this, he *behaved wisely* against Saul. He did not take matters into his own hands. Instead, he relied on the protective services that God provided. The Bible records that Saul eyed David and was envious of David. David understood those were not the only set of eyes that were watching him.

When it seems like things were not going in David's favor, he believed the plans of God. He knew that if he waited on the Lord, he would strengthen his heart and eventually give him the desires of his heart. He believed that his steps were being ordered by the Lord and the Lord delighted in them.

When you trust God's plan he will constantly provide. If He is your shepherd, you shall not want for anything!

To *behave wisely*, means that you walk with integrity and character. David believed that God honored faithfulness. He believed, "No good thing would he withhold from them that walk uprightly" (Psalm 84:11). Although we are not worthy of God's blessings, there are some benefits of walking upright and behaving wisely.

He Understood the Source Of His Success

The women were singing, "Saul has slain his thousands, and David his tens of thousands." They were singing the praises of David and were in awe of David's courage and bravery in battle. Those women were fans of his fighting capabilities. They were praising his strategies and success and were giving David the praise as their hero. There is danger in giving humans the credit that only God deserves. If we are not careful, we will begin to share God's glory. Compare their songs of praise with Exodus 15.

1 Then Moses and the Israelites sang this song to the Lord: "I will sing to the Lord, for he is highly exalted. The horse and its rider he has hurled into the sea. 2 The Lord is my strength and my song; he has become my salvation. He is my God, and I will praise him, my father's God, and I will exalt him.
3 The Lord is a warrior; the Lord is his name.
6 "Your right hand, O Lord, was majestic in power. Your right hand, O Lord, shattered the enemy. 7 In the greatness of your majesty you threw down those who opposed you.
11 "Who among the gods is like you, O Lord? Who is like you—majestic in holiness, awesome in glory, working wonders?
18 The Lord will reign for ever and ever."
(Exodus 15:1-3, 6-7, 11, 18 NIV)

David was able to behave wisely and handle the applause because he understood the source of his success. When David was preparing for battle with Goliath, he revealed the source of his success. He said in 1 Samuel 17:37, "The Lord who delivered me from the paw of the lion and the paw of the bear will deliver me from the hand of this Philistine." This attitude enabled him to handle the applause of the people. Although they were praising him, he knew it was not about him. We would do well to understand this principle. All the glory belongs to God.

We live in the age of "HERO WORSHIP" and Marvel Superheroes. We have made celebrities out of those called to be servants. We have developed leaders who would rather be popular rather than productive. Because of the applause and the attention, many leaders today have suffocated on their own success. They are enamored by fans, followers, friends, likes, retweets, views, mentions, and posts.

There is nothing wrong with spiritual success if we truly recognize the source behind the success. Scripture teaches that when we meditate on the word of God, we will have good success. So, although they were singing and shouting his praises, David knew that behaving wisely would bring about good success.

Humility Enables Us to Behave Wisely

6 Humble yourselves, therefore, under the mighty hand of God so that at the proper time he may exalt you,
(1 Peter 5:6 ESV)

Although David was the recipient of the applause of the people, he remained humbled in his service. David was a humble servant who put his trust and faith in God. As David's name begins to spread, he continued to rely on God's divine guidance. He saw no reason to exalt himself, but patiently awaited God to exalt him in due season. It was David who penned these words in Psalm 25:9, "He leads the humble in what is right, and teaches the humble his way." When we learn to walk in humility, God will honor our efforts. David was controlled by his spirit of humility. He was careful to avoid the snare of pride!

Although people revered him, women sang of his greatness, and thousands followed him into battle, David never forgot that he was just a shepherd boy that God chose to use. Instead of an ego, he exhibited humility. This can be seen in 1 Samuel 18 when Saul offered him his daughter. David responded by saying, "Who am I, and who are my relatives, my father's clan in Israel, that I should be son-in-law to the king?" Although his victories on the battlefield earned her hand in marriage, he still exhibited a spirit of humility. David is not as impressed with himself as others were.

Many people feel entitled, i.e. they deserve every blessing, every benefit, and every gift they receive. David understood that we are the beneficiaries of God's grace not deserving or worthy to receive. His humility contributed to his greatness as a leader. After David's ascension to the throne, he remained humbled under the mighty hand of God. In 2 Samuel 7:18, David responded to the announcement that his family shall sit on the throne forever by asking the question, "Who am I, O Lord God, and what is my house, that you have brought me thus far?" This is the model of humility.

David realized whose name carried real weight. Although the people were shouting his name, David understand there was a name that held all power. In Psalms 9:10, David says, "Those who know your name will trust in you…" There are those today who are seeking a name for themselves. Ministry leaders are consulting with branding experts to get noticed in a noisy world. They seek creative ways to stand out among the crowd.

The question becomes, "How can I brand my name?" Leaders are seeking the best approach to become influencers to promote "their name." This method is contrary to what Jesus exemplified. Paul shares with us in Philippians 2 that Jesus humbled himself and became obedient to death. Because of this obedience, God exalted Him and gave Him a name. We can behave wisely and handle the applause when we humble ourselves and allow God to exalt us in due season.

Reflect on this…

If you are not careful, a victory won

can turn around and defeat you.

Being successful can be dangerous if you

cannot handle the applause as well as the adversity.

Continue to Seek Fulfillment Rather Than Fanfare

Final Word

IT'S WORTH THE WAIT

³ Therefore all the elders of Israel came to the king at Hebron, and King David made a covenant with them at Hebron before the Lord. And they anointed David king over Israel. ⁴ David was thirty years old when he began to reign, and he reigned forty years.
(2 Samuel 5:3-4 NKJV)

After being anointed at the age of 17, David arrived at the place of promise. He had gone through the process to enjoy the fulfillment of "NOW." After the trials, after the tests, after the turmoil, after the troubles, it was FINALLY his turn. After serving faithfully under Saul, he FINALLY received his opportunity.

Have you been waiting on your turn? You have served others, you have celebrated others, you have supported others, you have encouraged others…

Now it's your turn.

It's your turn to lead,

It's your turn to make key decisions,

It's your turn to hold the power and position.

In 2003, Luther Barnes released a song that said, "You've been faithful, you've been true and you've done all that you can do, and for your faithfulness, it's your time. You applauded for the rest, now it's your time to be blessed, and for your faithfulness, it's your time."

Now, here is the crowning question: *Was It Worth The Wait?*

There were countless nights in the field with the sheep. There were continuous fleeing from an angry king. There was animosity, envy, and jealousy received all because of the anointing.

Was it worth the wait? I don't know if David agreed with the unknown author who wrote, "God has perfect timing: never early, never late. It takes a little patience and a whole lot of faith, but it's worth the wait."

Arriving At the Position Does Not Eliminate Problems

It didn't take long to discover that elevation to the position, does not eliminate the problems. In fact, they may be magnified. It might be your turn, but there will still be trouble. There are times when David probably thought; "this is not what I was expecting". After the coronation in 2 Samuel 5:1-5, verse 6 says, "And the king and his men went to Jerusalem against the Jebusites, the inhabitants of the land, who said to David, "You will not come in here, but the blind and the lame will ward you off"—thinking, "David cannot come in here."

Wait! On the heels of coronation, there is already conflict? We must remember, *Roses have Thorns*.

It's Worth the Wait

The Jebusites were only the beginning of the issues that David would face as King. Here is the list of problems faced:

- *The Jebusites taunted David's Ability to Conquer them (2 Samuel 5:6-10)*
- *The heated battle with the Philistines in the Valley of Rephaim (2 Samuel 5:17-25)*
- *Because of David's unwillingness to faithfully follow instructions; Uzzah died while bringing the ark back to Jerusalem (2 Samuel 6:6-8)*
- *The King had an adulterous affair with Bathsheba (2 Samuel 11:1-5)*
- *The king conspired to have Uriah, Bathsheba's husband killed in battle (2 Samuel 11:6-25)*
- *The king's son Amnon raped his own sister Tamar (2 Samuel 13)*
- *The king's son Absalom ordered his servants to kill his brother Amnon (2 Samuel 13:31)*
- *The king's son Absalom sought to usurp his father's authority and take the throne (2 Samuel 16 -18)*
- *Sheba, the Benjamite, lead a revolt against the king (2 Samuel 20)*
- *The king displeased God by numbering the people (2 Samuel 24:1-4)*
- *The land is plagued because of sin and 70,000 died (2 Samuel 24:15)*
- *In his old age, his son, Adonijah seeks to become king instead of Solomon (1 Kings 1:5)*

I ask again… *was it worth the wait?* After coronation, there seems to be seasons filled with constant chaos, family conflict and enemies that must be conquered. Was this part of God's plan? Did David wait thirteen years for more trials, tribulations, and turbulence? Was the purpose of going through trouble really to get into a better position to receive more trouble?

After being installed as a new pastor, I envisioned a road of perfect harmony. I was leading a growing congregation. We were growing numerically, spiritually, and financially. Then adversity arose from within and without. We experienced conflict among some leaders that splintered the church. I remember reading the question that John the Baptist asked in Matthew 11, "Are you the one or should we look for someone else."

What I was experiencing as leader did not match what I expected. I did not expect these problems once I received the position. I was beginning to develop the mindset of the children of God in the wilderness, Should I have stayed in Egypt? Did you bring me here to perish in the position? Then I remembered, I was prepared for such a time as this!

PREPARED FOR SUCH A TIME AS THIS

"For if you remain silent at this time, relief and deliverance for the Jews will arise from another place, but you and your father's family will perish. And who knows but that you have come to royal position for such a time as this?"
(Esther 4:14 NIV)

God prepares his leaders to stand in times of crisis. Esther had to be reminded that her elevation to the royal position was not for personal profit or pleasure; but for such a time as this. We will discover that David's thirteen years of training was preparing him for such a time as this!

God had placed David in the waiting room for thirteen years to learn how to respond to trouble. He learned to handle crisis, love his enemies, serve faithfully, and honor authority in the wilderness while he was waiting on God. In the wilderness, God had proved Himself faithful time and time again. Now David's confidence in God was unshakeable.

Receive the *Teaching Time*

David learned to trust God during the process. So many people want to eliminate the process and get to the position. In the process, David learned to nourish, protect, and guide his father's sheep. He learned to be a dependable shepherd. Once he was exalted, he was still a shepherd. The only difference was the flock.

God may not allow you to leave the waiting room until you have learned some things. In the process, David learned a few things

- *Learned to Trust in the Lord {Psalm 37:3}*
- *Learned to Delight in The Lord {Psalm 37:4}*
- *Learned to Commit his ways To The Lord {Psalm 37:5}*
- *Learned to Rest in the Lord {Psalm 37:7}*
- *Learned to Wait on the Lord {Psalm 37:34}*

Accept the *Testing Time*

> "*² Consider it pure joy, my brothers, whenever you face trials of many kinds, ³ because you know that the testing of your faith develops perseverance. ⁴ Perseverance must finish its work so*

> *that you may be mature and complete,*
> *not lacking anything.*
> (James 1:2-4 NIV)

It is important to note that there are two different types of tests we will receive. We must pass both to progress on our spiritual journey. One of those tests is to measure the content of your knowledge. This is a *Head Test*.

The other kind of test measures the content of our character. This is the *Test of the Heart*. Sometimes the tests we must face will have to do with knowledge and information. Other times they will have more to do with our character and our moral convictions. To put it another way, some exams are designed to find out what you know. Other exams that are designed to find out "Who you are?"

Testing brings validity and credibility in the secular. Testing brings validity and credibility in the spiritual. God gives tests to bring validity to your values and credibility to your character.

Prepare for the *Test of Elevation*

> 5 *"If you have raced with men on foot and they have worn you out, how can you compete with horses? If you stumble in safe country, how will you manage in the thickets by the Jordan?"*
> (Jeremiah 12:5 NIV)

As we are faithful in every test, God will give us a larger range of responsibility. In almost every area of your life there comes a moment when you must take a test, an examination of some sort, and the results of that test determine whether you can continue along the path you are following. Students must pass proficiency exams in school before they can proceed to higher levels of learning. There is a test required for any profession or vocation you may want to pursue. Whether you want to be a barber, a physician, a lawyer, or an engineer there comes a moment when you must take and pass a test before you can proceed any further. It does not matter what you do for a living or what you are aspiring to do some day, it is almost a certainty that there are some exams and tests you will have to pass before you can proceed to the Next Level.

David was found to be faithful with his father's sheep. He protected the sheep from the bears and the lions. He provided the proper nourishment for his father's sheep. Therefore, he was elevated into Saul's court. Despite the animosity and adversity he faced, he was a faithful musician, leader, and warrior in Saul's court. He was loyal, diligent, and devoted to serving the king. Therefore, he was elevated to the king of one tribe, Judah. He was not elevated to the king of all Israel, ***only Judah.***

As king of Judah, David faced challenges from the house of Saul. We are told that David grew stronger with every test. We read, "Now there was a long war between the house of Saul and the house of David; and David grew steadily stronger, but the house of Saul grew weaker continually" (2 Samuel 3:1). Because he stood strong in the time of testing, finally he was elevated to king of Israel. God will test your skills and capacity to handle adversity before giving elevation.

Face the *Test of Character*

"3 Not only so, but we also rejoice in our sufferings, because we know that suffering produces perseverance;
4 perseverance, character; and character, hope."
(Romans 5:3-4 NIV)

Christians have access to the knowledge and wisdom that makes it possible to face and endure trials. David knew that the sufferings, trials, and tests were designed to produce something inside him to impact things around him. He was able to deal with the problems in the position because of what God had produced in him through the process. The process produced perseverance, character, and hope. For this reason, we must find joy in the journey and not just the destination.

We know that the journey produces perseverance or staying power. Many people panic and flee at the first sign of opposition. The journey enables us to stick with it knowing God has a plan and a purpose based on the promise. The Promise to David was, "I am anointing you to be the next king." When David wanted to give up, the promise enabled him to persevere through the process.

We know the journey produces character. This gives the idea of being approved. God develops our character through the testing of our faith. You do not really know what you are made of until you have been proven by God. The people put Saul in the position, but he was not able to stay until he was approved by God. Many people have positions but the lack the character to succeed.

Finally, David knew that the journey produced hope. Hope is a bold, confident expectation. Hope believes that God has something better on the other side of your trials, tests, and temptations. Hope looks beyond the current situation to the joy ahead. David was confident looking ahead because of the trials God had brought him through in the past. Hope does not disappoint. When David looked in the rear-view mirror, he had enough evidence to strengthen his expectation in God. David had challenges in his position as king, but he maintained his expectation. In

Psalm 39:7 he cries out… "And now, Lord, for what do I wait? My hope is in You." *David did not put his hope in people, positions, policies, or practices. He put his hope in God.*

You can find joy and fulfillment in the journey toward your destination if you learn to maximize your time until it is your turn. It may not seem like you will succeed while going through the journey but know that the testing of your faith is producing something in you.

Now, Thank God for the Journey

A songwriter stated, "I thank God for the mountains, and I thank Him for the valleys, I thank Him for the storms He brought me through. For if I never had a problem, I would not know God could solve them; I would never know what faith in God could do. Through it all, I learned to trust in God; through it all, I learned to depend upon his word." Amen.

About the Author

Dr. Marcus L. Ellison serves as Senior Pastor of the Mt. Olive Baptist Church of Greenwood. He is a native of Farmerville, Louisiana. Dr. Ellison is married to the love of his life, TaSheka Morris-Ellison, and they are the proud parents of one daughter, Morgan LaDawn Ellison.

Dr. Ellison has a strong desire to study and teach the Word of God. He is a strong advocate for higher learning. He received a Bachelor of Arts in Religion from the B.M.A. Theological Seminary in Jacksonville, TX in 2009 and a Master of Arts in Religion from B.M.A. in 2010. Dr. Ellison later received a Master of Divinity and Doctor of Ministry from Liberty Theological Seminary in Lynchburg, VA.

Dr. Ellison is grateful for the opportunity that God has given him to serve as Pastor/Teacher of the Mt. Olive B.C. of Greenwood, La. His motto is "To Whom Much Is Given, Much Is Required."

Endnotes

[1] John C. Maxwell, *The 360° Leader* (Nashville, TN: Thomas Nelson Publishing, 2011), 4.

[2] Daniel Threlfall, "Pastoral Promotion: How Climbing Up Will Take You Down," *ShareFaith* (August 2011).

[3] Billy Hornsby, *Success for the Second in Command* (Lake Mary, FL: Creation House Publishing, 2004), 10.

[4] David W. Hopewell, *Keys to Becoming an Effective Associate Minister and Church Leader* (Lithonia, GA: Orman Press, 2004), 32.

[5] Martin E. Hawkins, *The Associate Pastor: Second Chair, Not Second Best* (Nashville, TN: Broadman amp and Holman Publishers, 2005), 21.

[6] Hopewell, *Keys to Becoming*.

[7] J. Robert Clinton, *The Making of a Leader* (Colorado Springs, CO: Navpress Publishing, 1988), 23.

[8] David Hopewell, Keys to Becoming an Effective Associate Minister (Lithonia, GA: Orman Press Inc., 2004, 29)

[9] Joseph Walker, "No Opportunity Wasted, The Art of Execution" (Nashville, TN: Heritage Publishing, 2017), 35.

[10] https://hbcharlesjr.com/resource-library/articles/help-im-an-associate-ministers/

[11] https://www.christianquotes.info/quotes-by-topic/quotes-about-patience/

[12] https://jameslongjr.org/patience-in-delays-and-detours/

[13] https://www.awakenthegreatnesswithin.com/35-inspirational-quotes-on-patience/

[14] Dr. Larry Keefauver, *77 Irrefutable Truths of Ministry,* © 2019

www.ingramcontent.com/pod-product-compliance
Lightning Source LLC
Chambersburg PA
CBHW060848050426
42453CB00008B/893